NATURAL WORLD

ORANGUTAN

HABITATS • LIFE CYCLES • FOOD CHAINS • THREATS

Stephen Brend

HODDER
Wayland

an imprint of Hodder
Children's Books

WWF

Produced in Association with WWF-UK

NATURAL WORLD

Chimpanzee • Crocodile • Dolphin • Elephant
Giant Panda • Great White Shark • Grizzly Bear
Hippopotamus • Killer Whale • Lion • Orangutan
Penguin • Polar Bear • Tiger

Produced for Hodder Wayland by
Roger Coote Publishing
Gissing's Farm, Fressingfield
Suffolk IP21 5SH, UK

WWF is a registered charity no. 201707
WWF-UK, Panda House, Weyside Park
Godalming, Surrey GU7 1XR

Cover photo: Eye to eye with an adult male orangutan.
Title page: A young orangutan.
Contents page: Orangutans are excellent climbers.
Index page: Just hanging around in the tree-tops.

Editor: Steve Setford
Series editor: Polly Goodman
Designer: Sarah Crouch
Cover designer: Victoria Webb

Published in Great Britain in 2000 by Hodder Wayland,
an imprint of Hodder Children's Books

A Catalogue record for this book is available from the
British Library.

ISBN 0 7502 2690 0

Printed and bound by G. Canale & C. S.p.A. Turin, Italy

Hodder Children's Books
A division of Hodder Headline plc
338 Euston Road, London NW1 3BH

Picture credits
Stephen Brend/IPPL 41; Bruce Coleman Collection *front cover* (John Cancalosi), 3 (Jorg and Petra Wegner), 9 (Erwin and Peggy Bauer), 11 (Christer Fredriksson), 13 (Christer Fredriksson), 15 (Gerald S. Cubitt), 17 (Christer Fredriksson), 18 (Michael P. Price), 21 (Ingo Arndt), 23, 25 (Alain Compost), 26 (Christer Fredriksson), 27, 29 (Alain Compost), 31 (Christer Fredriksson), 32, 33 (Alain Compost), 35 (John Cancalosi), 40 (Alain Compost), 44 middle (Christer Fredriksson), 45 middle, 45 bottom (Alain Compost). Digital Vision 7, 36, 37, 48; NHPA 1 (Mark Bowler), 8, 10 (B. Jones and M. Shimlock), 19 (Mark Bowler), 30 (John Shaw), 38 (Daniel Heuclin), 39 (Andy Rouse), 42, 43 (Martin Harvey), 44 top (B. Jones and M. Shimlock); The Orangutan Foundation 34 (Ian Redmond); Oxford Scientific Films 12 (Mike Hill), 14, 16 (Konrad Wothe), 24 (Michael Dick), 28 (Mike Hill), 44 bottom (Konrad Wothe); Still Pictures 22, 45 top (Cyril Rouso). Maps on page 4 by Victoria Webb and Peter Bull. All other artworks by Michael Posen.

Contents

Meet the Orangutan 4

An Orangutan is Born 8

Growing Up 12

Leaving Home 22

Daily Life 26

Adulthood 30

Threats 36

Orangutan Life Cycle 44

Topic Web 46

Extension Activities 46

Glossary 47

Further Information 47

Index 48

Meet the Orangutan

Orangutans are the world's largest tree-dwelling mammals. They live on the islands of Borneo and Sumatra, up in the rainforest canopy, descending to the forest floor only to eat. Their eyes, facial expressions and the way they move their hands are so human-like it is not surprising that their name means 'person of the forest' in the Malay language.

◀ Indonesia's position in the world.

▲ The red shading on this map shows where orangutans live.

ORANGUTAN FACTS

There are two species of orangutan: the Bornean and the Sumatran. The scientific name for the Bornean orangutan is *pongo pygmaeus* and for the Sumatran, *pongo abelii*.

●

Adult males can reach 1.5 metres in height and can weigh as much as 100 kilograms. Females are much smaller. They are about 1 metre tall and weigh up to 45 kilograms.

▼ An adult male orangutan.

Arms

Orangutans' arms are immensely strong and can be more than 1 metre long. This helps them to climb and to reach fruit that might be at the end of a branch too small to hold the animal's weight.

Eyes

The forward-facing eyes enable orangutans to judge distances accurately. The eyes are dark-brown, because the bright tropical sunlight would damage lighter-coloured eyes.

Cheek pads

Adult males develop huge face pads, which are often covered with scars and bite marks from fights with rival males.

Throat pouch

Males inflate the pouch to make their calls carry further. When it is not inflated, it hangs down like a double chin.

Hands

Like humans, orangutan hands have a separate thumb that sits opposite four fingers. This is called an opposable thumb, and it enables them to hold and move objects. The thick fingers have fingerprints.

Coat

The orangutan's hair is usually red, but the colour can vary greatly. Some, for example, may be dark-brown, while others are almost blond.

Feet

Orangutans' feet are more like an extra pair of hands because they use them mainly for climbing.

The Great Apes

Orangutans are a type of great ape. The great apes are a group of mammals that all have large brains, gripping hands and forward-pointing eyes. Gorillas, chimpanzees and bonobos are also great apes. In fact, scientists classify humans as great apes too. Besides humans, orangutans are the only great apes found outside Africa.

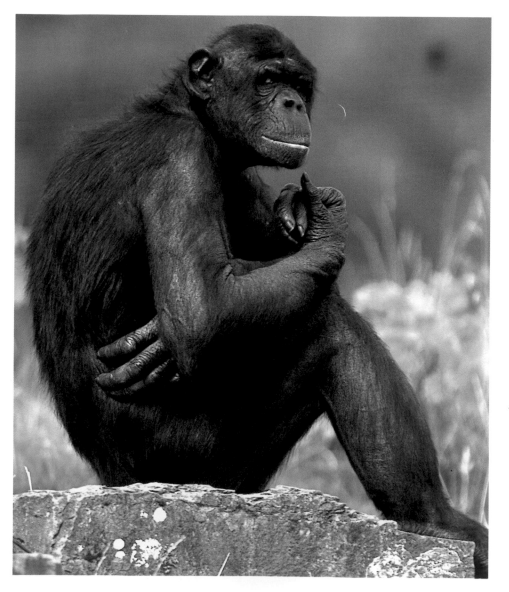

◀ The bonobo, or pygmy chimpanzee, is the smallest of the great apes. It lives in large family groups, called troops, in the rain forests of the Congo River Basin, in Central Africa.

Gorillas, chimpanzees and bonobos sleep in trees, but they mainly move on the ground, whereas orangutans spend almost all their time in the trees. The African great apes live in groups, and the groups may form part of a larger community. Orangutans are solitary, and mostly live alone.

Orangutans live on the Indonesian islands of Borneo and Sumatra, in rain forests made up of tall, straight trees called diterocarps. Orangutans also live in swamp forests, which can become flooded after heavy rain. This makes the ability to move through the trees essential.

▲ Chimpanzees are humans' closest relatives in the animal kingdom. They are more closely related to humans than they are to orangutans.

7

An Orangutan is Born

Orangutan mothers give birth at night to a single baby, after an eight or nine-month pregnancy. Very occasionally, a female orangutan may have twins. The mother is alone in her nest during the birth, but there may be an older son or daughter sleeping nearby. Once the baby is born, the mother cleans the infant and raises it to her breast so that it can suckle for the first time.

▲ A new-born orangutan is totally dependent on its mother. It cannot even raise its head. Within two weeks, it will have learnt how to sit upright and use its hands.

The orangutan mother carries her baby, clutching it to her chest as she moves through the forest. Even though she has such a small baby, the mother continues to spend most of her time in the tree-tops, with the baby clinging on up to 30 metres above the ground.

▼ A mother orangutan is very protective towards her baby. For the first two years of its life, a baby orangutan is in constant physical contact with its mother.

BABY ORANGUTANS

A baby orangutan weighs about 1.5 kilograms when it is born. Its eyes are open at birth and it very quickly learns to use its fingers to grip, but it is still totally dependent on its mother.

•

The baby has big eyes, a very large head and a very thin coat of hair. The arms and legs are thin, because their muscles only start to develop once the orangutan begins climbing trees.

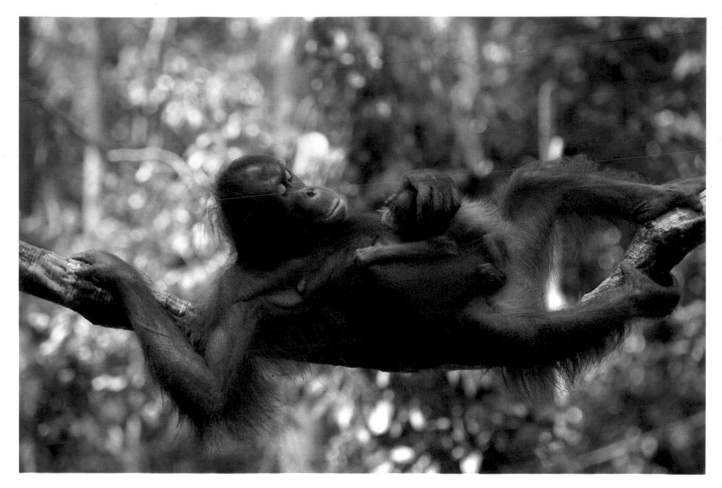

The bond between a female orangutan and her baby is the strongest of all relationships in orangutan society. The females are very good mothers and will do anything to care for and protect their young.

The mother carries her baby for the first year of its life. As the baby gets stronger, it will start to hold on by itself, either on its mother's chest or on her back. One of the reasons a mother carries her baby for so long is that she does not want to risk the baby falling if it tries to climb by itself.

▲ A mother clutches her young baby to her chest as she rests on a branch. When the baby is older, it will start to ride on its mother's back.

The mother watches out for predators. Adults have few natural enemies, but tigers occasionally attack them and pigs have been known to kill orangutan babies. Orangutans are only in danger when they are on the ground, which is another reason for spending so much time in the trees.

▼ The Sumatran tiger is Indonesia's largest predator. It will attack orangutans, but they often manage to escape by climbing into the trees.

Growing Up

◀ This baby is still living off its mother's milk. It will soon start tasting her food and learning what fruits are good to eat.

When it is about three months' old, the baby orangutan begins eating soft fruit, as well as drinking its mother's milk. Sometimes the baby drinks water from its mother's mouth, or tastes some of her food.

The baby will not begin to move about by itself until it is at least one year old. Even then it will still be carried by its mother for much of the time and will continue to sleep in her nest.

Occasionally, two females will meet and spend some time together feeding. If both the females have babies, the babies will play together while their mothers eat.

▼ Perched on its mother's shoulders, a young orangutan is carried across a river. Orangutans cannot swim, so they usually avoid wading through water by swinging across rivers using nearby trees.

As a juvenile, the young orangutan will no longer share its mother's night nest and must build its own. This young orangutan has built its night nest in a bamboo thicket.

Learning About Life

The mother begins to wean the young orangutan when it is three to four years old. At this age it is called a juvenile. Weaning can be a stressful time, with the juvenile screaming and throwing tantrums.

BUILDING A NIGHT NEST

Night nests are made by bending twigs over and weaving them together. The orangutan begins by making a circular platform. It then lines the platform with leaves and twigs. It can take up to 30 minutes to build a night nest from start to finish.

•

Young orangutans practise building nests from an early age, so that by the time they leave their mother's nest, they can make their own perfectly.

The orangutan youngster starts to build its own night nests at about this age. They will always be close to the mother's nest, perhaps even in the same tree. As it travels around with its mother, the young orangutan learns about which foods are found where and at what time of year. It also learns how high it is safe to climb, how to move quickly through the trees, and all about the different forest sounds.

Sometimes the mother and juvenile encounter an adult male, who inspects the mother to see if she is ready to mate. The juvenile may be scared because the males are so large. Occasionally, the mother and juvenile will be accompanied by an older, adolescent orangutan that has left its own mother. These meetings teach the juvenile how to behave towards other orangutans.

▼ This orangutan can now climb by itself and use its hands and feet to hold food.

A Growing Family

The orangutan mother becomes pregnant again after mating with an adult male. She must make sure that the juvenile is completely weaned off her milk before she gives birth again. Pregnancy is a very dangerous time for her, because if food is not plentiful she may become very weak. The new-born infant is totally dependent on its mother, who has to feed both herself and her baby.

The arrival of a brother or sister forces the juvenile into second place. The new baby is the mother's first concern, so the juvenile must start to look after itself. But it may well travel with its mother and her new baby.

▶ Orangutans use their feet like an extra pair of hands, holding on to trees and vines as they move through the forest.

▼ Orangutans get a lot of the water they need from the fruits that they eat, but they will also drink from rivers and streams. Young orangutans enjoy playing with water.

Finding Food

Orangutans depend on rain to find enough food. Tropical rain is very heavy. It comes in long storms called monsoons, which flood the swamp forests and make travelling on the ground almost impossible. The forest trees need the rain to produce flowers and fruit.

Different forest trees produce fruit at different times of the year, and if there is not enough rain at the right time, some fruits may be scarce. The orangutans may have to go hungry for many months until another fruit comes into season.

▼ When it rains, orangutans will cover their heads with large leaves or seek shelter. The huge roots at the base of a tree give some shelter to this damp youngster, but orangutans do not usually rest on the forest floor.

Orangutans find food partly by remembering where they found it last, but also by scent and exploration. The orangutans must balance the quality of the food against the amount of time it takes to find it. Bark and leaves are plentiful and available all year round, but they are not very nutritious and are difficult for the orangutans to digest. Seasonal fruits and flower nectar, which contain sugar, are sometimes harder to find, but they supply more energy and can be more easily absorbed by the body.

▲ The young orangutan learns which foods are good to eat by watching its mother.

An Orangutan's Diet

Although orangutans eat more than 400 different plants, or parts of plants, 90 per cent of their diet consists of fruit. They are especially fond of a fruit called a durian. To a human nose, durians smell horrible, but orangutans love them!

▼ Orangutans eat a variety of foods, from energy-rich fruits, seeds and nectar to less-nutritious bark and leaves. They will also feed on insects, and will occasionally catch and eat small mammals such as mice and lorises.

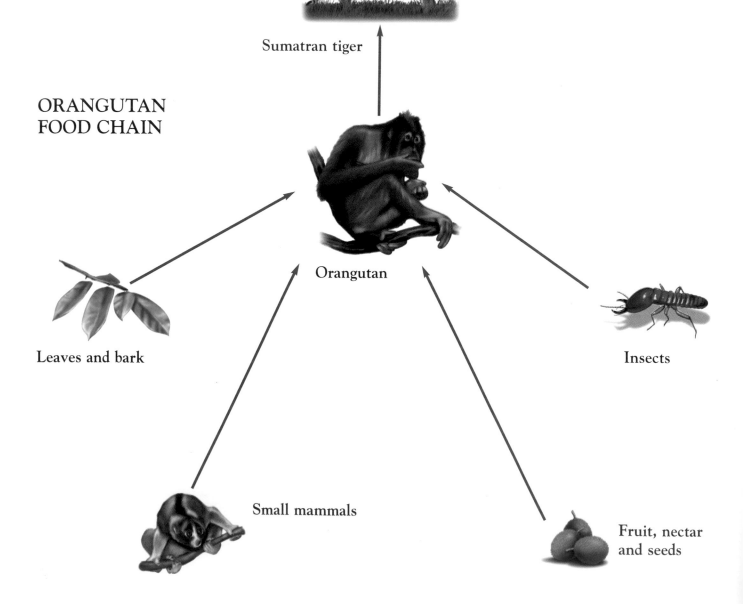

ORANGUTAN
FOOD CHAIN

Sumatran tiger

Orangutan

Leaves and bark

Insects

Small mammals

Fruit, nectar and seeds

Orangutans also eat flower nectar, honey, bark, leaves, termites and fungi. They balance their diets just like people, making sure they get a mixture of sugars and fats (from fruit), carbohydrates (from leaves) and protein (from nuts). They sometimes eat mice and other small mammals, but meat does not seem to be very important to them.

▼ This orangutan has broken a piece off a termites' nest and is trying to fish out the insects with its tongue.

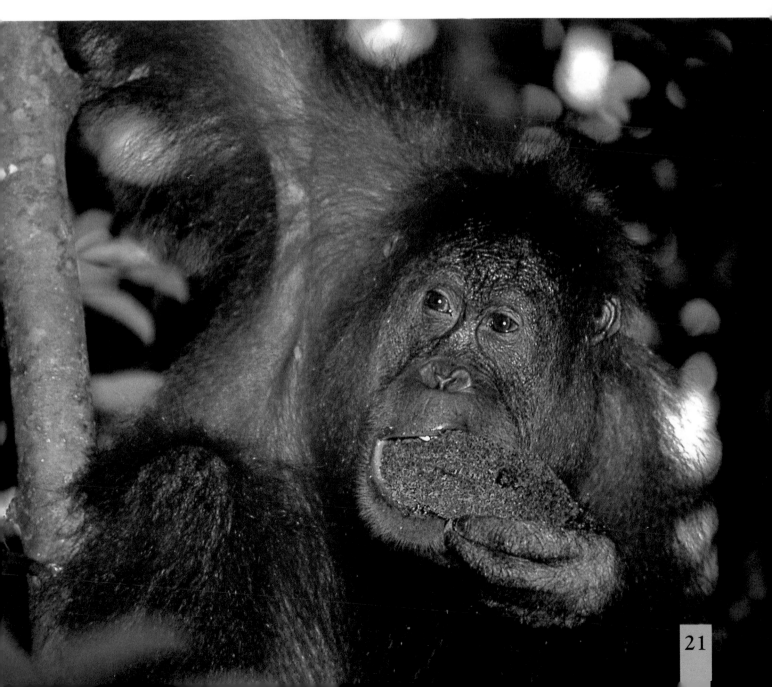

Leaving Home

By the time it is five or six years old, the orangutan has become an adolescent. It begins to spend longer and longer away from its mother and her second-born child. Sometimes the adolescent moves around the forest alone, but at other times it travels with other females and their babies. It is becoming increasingly independent.

▼ This adolescent male is yawning, showing the developing canine teeth at the corners of his jaws. Orangutans use these teeth for cracking nuts. The males also use them for fighting.

▶ The young orangutan will stay with its mother until it is six or seven years old. Then it will start to explore the forest on its own, before becoming fully independent.

A young male orangutan may show some sexual interest in these females, but his advances will always be rejected. It will be another three or four years before he is accepted as an adult. Female orangutans are lighter than males. They can flee from an adolescent male by moving into the higher, smaller branches of a tree, which will not hold the heavier adolescent.

The adolescent continues to learn social behaviour from these encounters, discovering for itself the signs that other orangutans make to show what mood they are in.

Proboscis monkeys are famous for their long noses. Like orangutans, they eat mainly fruit, but orangutans are larger than proboscis monkeys and will push them away from the best fruit trees.

Sharing the Forest

During its wanderings, the adolescent will also encounter other animals that live in the rain forest. Indonesia's rain forests are home to eagles, swifts, hornbills and many other birds. There are also reptiles, such as snakes and crocodiles, and many mammals, including leopards, bats, porcupines and proboscis monkeys. There are also thousands of insect species.

When it is about seven years old, the orangutan leaves its mother and becomes independent. Now it is called a sub-adult. A female sub-adult may share part of the area where her mother lives, called her home range, but a young male will move further away from his birthplace.

Fully adult males will not tolerate a young male nearby, so he must set off to find a home range of his own, which he can defend against male rivals.

▶ As males start to become sub-adults, they begin to develop cheek pads. Sumatran males, such as this one, may also grow shaggy beards.

Daily Life

All orangutans travel through the trees, moving from branch to branch and from trunk to trunk. They can walk along the thickest branches. To move from one branch to another, or between trees, orangutans use their feet like hands. They hold the first branch as they reach out to test the strength of the next branch. If the gap between the branches is too great, they will rock one branch so that it swings closer to the next one.

Occasionally, orangutans miss a handhold and fall. But because they are very strong and agile, they can usually break their fall by grabbing on to other, stronger branches. On rare occasions they may tumble all the way to the ground. A fall may injure or even kill a young orangutan, but adults are usually only bruised.

▶ Unlike females, adult males may travel on the ground since some trees are not strong enough to take their weight. They usually walk on clenched fists, but they can walk upright if they need to.

▶ The long arms of an orangutan help it to reach from one tree to another, but adult males like this one will not climb too high on such small trees.

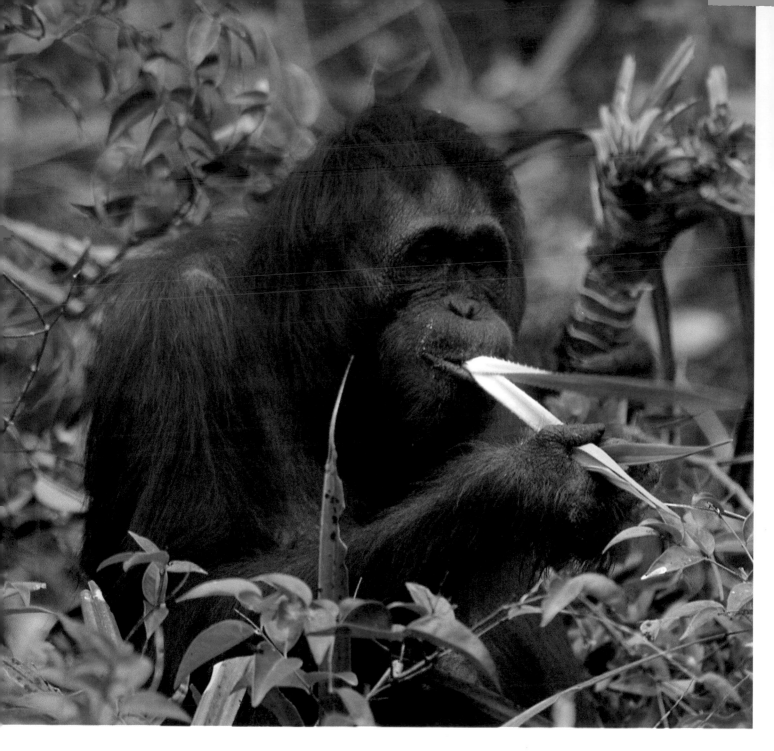

An Orangutan's Day

The way orangutans spend their day depends on how much food is available. In total, they may spend up to six hours feeding or looking for food. If fruit is plentiful, they will take the opportunity to gorge themselves.

▲ The orangutan's teeth and jaws are very powerful. The orangutan strips leaves off branches by dragging them through its mouth.

Orangutans wake at dawn and leave their night nests to begin looking for food. Most days, they travel only between 600 and 850 metres from their nest, moving from one food source to another depending upon which fruits are in season. They will visit the same tree again and again until all its fruit is gone.

After a morning's feeding, orangutans build day nests, which are smaller than night nests. They rest in their day nests while they digest their food. Then in the afternoon, they feed again, either returning to the same tree or moving to a new one.

▼ A sub-adult orangutan resting in its day nest.

Adulthood

Orangutan females reach adulthood earlier than males. Females become fully mature and capable of breeding at around seven years of age, although they rarely have their first baby until they are nine or ten.

Male orangutans are not fully mature until they are at least ten years old. When a male has established his own territory and is able to breed with females, he develops cheek pads.

▼ A male's cheek pads let females know that he is old enough to breed, and probably help to scare away rival males. The cheek pads may also help the male orangutan to make his loud, booming calls.

The area where an orangutan lives is known as its home range. A male's range is usually large, possibly up to 7 square kilometres. There may be several females within a male's range, and the females' ranges may overlap. A female's home range only has to enclose enough food for her and her young. A male's range, on the other hand, must enclose females with whom he can mate, as well as his own food supply.

Young adult males that do not stay in one area but travel widely throughout the forest are called wanderers. Scientists are not sure whether these males eventually settle down when they find an unoccupied area, or whether they spend all their adult lives as wanderers.

▼ Male orangutans will fight to keep other males away from the females in their home ranges. You can see the fully developed canine teeth in this Sumatran male.

◄ This huge Bornean male is in the prime of his life. He is at least 25 years old and probably weighs over 90 kilograms.

ORANGUTAN NOISES

Dominant males make a booming 'long call' by inflating their throat pouches. It lasts for up to three minutes and can be heard up to a kilometre away. Males use this call to mark out their territory and to attract females.

●

The fast call is similar to the long call, but has a faster note. It is used as a threat.

●

Annoyed orangutans purse their lips and make a smacking noise called a kiss-squeak.

Courtship and Breeding

Mating can take place at any time of year. It depends on whether the female is ready to become pregnant and if she likes the dominant male. This is the time when male orangutans are most likely to fight, as each tries to gain access to the female.

If a male meets a willing female and she accepts him, he will court her. During courtship the pair move around the forest together, sharing food, remaining close to one another and often touching. The courtship period may be very short, sometimes lasting little more than a day.

Mating may occur many times during the courtship and can occur on the ground, in the trees or even hanging from a branch. Once courtship and mating are over, the male leaves the female and he takes no further part in the birth or rearing of his baby.

Female orangutans continue to breed throughout their adult lives, but they usually only have three or four young in their lifetime. This slow breeding rate makes it difficult for orangutan numbers to increase.

▶ A female orangutan in Sumatra.

33

Old age

Orangutans have long lives, sometimes reaching over 50 years of age. Some orangutans die prematurely from illness and disease. Others may die from starvation if food is particularly scarce. They have no natural predators apart from tigers and leopards, which sometimes kill adult females.

Old orangutans prefer to avoid meeting others and are rarely seen in the wild. Old males are probably too weak to fight, so they may give up their territory to younger orangutans.

▶ An old female orangutan. Like the males, female orangutans gradually become slower and weaker as they get older.

▼ An adult male's cheek pads may be scarred and torn as a result of fighting with other males.

Threats

Unfortunately, the orangutan is not safe in its forest world. Its numbers have fallen by about 80 per cent since 1900. No one is quite sure how many orangutans are left in the wild, but estimates range from 15,000 to 20,000.

The main threat to Indonesia's orangutans is the destruction of their rainforest habitat. The forest trees are being cut down for timber and the land is being cleared for mining. As new settlements spring up, more forest is turned into farmland.

▼ The wood from tropical trees is very valuable. This encourages people to cut the trees down for timber. People then use the land for farming, making it impossible for the forest to recover.

In 1997, raging fires swept through the orangutans' forests. The fires were deliberately started by people who wanted the land for farming, but they got out of control and spread rapidly. The fires burnt for more than a month and destroyed over 1,000 square kilometres of forest.

▲ While the tallest and strongest trees may survive a fire, most of the forest is destroyed and many of the animals that live in it are killed.

The Indonesian government is aware of the problems the orangutans face. It has made some forest areas into national parks and wildlife reserves, where the orangutans can live in their habitat undisturbed by human activity.

The Pet Trade

In some countries, people like to keep baby orangutans as pets. To capture a baby, hunters must first shoot its mother. This is very disturbing to the infant and it is quite likely to die of shock.

Even if the young orphan survives being captured, it may die on its way to its new owner. Because it is illegal to take orangutans out of Indonesia, they must be smuggled out, often in small crates or packages with false labels.

▼ Many people think young apes are cute. This young chimpanzee and orangutan are being raised together as pets, but the pet trade threatens both species.

The few orangutans that survive the journey face a difficult life. People only like to keep them as pets when they are small, but once an orangutan has grown larger and stronger, it may be abandoned or sold into a bad zoo. All conservation organizations agree that orangutans are not suitable to keep as pets and there is an international effort to stop this trade.

▲ Because they are intelligent, orangutans can be taught to perform many tricks. Like the pet trade, collecting animals for circuses threatens wild populations.

39

Orangutan Conservation

Some orangutans live in zoos that look after them well and try to make their lives as natural as possible. This is difficult, because few zoos have access to all the wild fruits that an orangutan would normally eat. Also, wild orangutans usually live alone, but in zoos they are forced to live with other orangutans.

▼ Many orangutans are kept in zoos around the world. Now that orangutans have bred successfully in captivity, it is no longer necessary for zoos to collect more animals from the wild.

Despite this, many orangutans have got used to living with each other in zoos and have managed to breed successfully. Breeding in zoos is called captive breeding. Some people believe captive breeding plays an important part in conservation, because it helps to maintain orangutan numbers at a time when some wild populations are threatened with extinction. However, others think it is better to return orangutans to the wild than breed them in captivity.

Zoos also play an important role in educating the public. What better way to learn about orangutans than seeing how they behave face to face?

▲ This orangutan orphan will have to live in captivity until he is old enough to be released back into the wild. While he is in captivity, he needs to be fed as natural a diet as possible.

Rehabilitation

Some orangutans have been returned to the wild in a process called rehabilitation. Many of these orangutans were once pets. Others were confiscated from smugglers, and some were orphaned when their mothers were killed in forest fires.

In the wild, the orphans' mothers would have taught them the skills they needed, such as how to make a night nest and what fruits to eat. Without their mothers, the baby orangutans must learn from people. Rehabilitation centres are usually located in national parks, where the orangutans will be safe from hunters when they are released.

▲ These orangutans are at a rehabilitation centre. They are not used to finding their own fruit in the trees, so the wardens at the centre give them extra food. Once the orangutans have learnt to fend for themselves in the wild, they will no longer need this extra food.

DISEASE

Orangutans can catch many human diseases. This can be a problem, because orangutans' bodies are not used to our diseases, so they suffer more than we do.

●

Rehabilitation centres are very careful to ensure that sickness does not spread between orphans and, most importantly, from orphans to the wild population. Quarantine is the name given to the process of keeping sick animals away from healthy ones.

Most rehabilitated orangutans only become semi-wild, and occasionally return to the rehabilitation centre to feed. However, a few do become truly wild and spend the rest of their lives in the forest. Many tourists come to the rehabilitation centres to see orangutans. This helps to pay for the orphans' food and the wages of the national park wardens, who protect the wild orangutans and their forest home.

You will find a list of wildlife groups trying to help orangutans on page 47.

▼ Orangutans must be fit and healthy before they are returned to the forest. The youngsters are weighed regularly to check that they are growing normally.

Orangutan Life Cycle

 1 A single baby orangutan is born after an eight- or nine-month pregnancy. The mother is alone when she gives birth. The baby suckles its mother's milk.

 2 The baby begins to eat solid food after three or four months, but it continues to suckle for another three years. For the first year of its life, it is carried everywhere by its mother.

 3 When the orangutan is four years old and a juvenile, its mother weans it off her milk. Females may give birth every four or five years.

4 Aged five or six, the adolescent orangutan begins to spend more time away from its mother and her second baby. Occasionally, it may travel with another female and her baby.

5 By seven years of age, the orangutan is a sub-adult and independent. A sub-adult female may live near its mother, but a male sub-adult moves further away.

6 Female orangutans have their first baby at about ten years old. Males are not fully adult until they are almost fourteen. They develop huge cheek pads and become the dominant male in a territory. Orangutans can live for more than fifty years.

GEOGRAPHY
- Mapwork: where orangutans live
- Environmental change and deforestation
- Seasons and weather
- Floods
- Ecotourism

ART
- Camouflage patterns
- Leaf patterns
- Orangutan masks

SCIENCE
- Rainforest habitat
- Classification: great apes
- Adaptation and evolution
- Life cycle of the orangutan
- Life cycle of the diterocarp tree.
- Food chains
- Parts of the body
- Protection of environment
- Interdependence of plants and animals

Orangutan Topic Web

MATHS
- Orangutan numbers
- Height and weight comparisons
- Calendar in an orangutan's year

ENGLISH & LITERACY
- Conservation debates
- Rainforest myths and legends

ICT
- Search for conservation groups' website
- Write an email to a zoo

Extension Activities

English
- Debate the motion: 'Zoos help the conservation of orangutans'.
- Find and list collective names for groups of animals, or terms for their young, e.g. pup, cub, baby.
- Write a letter to a conservation group expressing a point of view.

Geography
- Trace a world map from an atlas. Show the location of rain forests and Indonesia.
- Draw a great ape distribution map.
- Draw maps of different scales: Borneo, Indonesia and the world.

Maths
- Compare the numbers of endangered species around the world, e.g. compare orangutans to tigers.
- Compare heights and weights of orangutans to chimpanzees.

Science
- Make a list of body parts that humans and orangutans share.
- Make a chart showing how parts of the orangutan's body are specially adapted for certain functions.
- Discuss the effect of monsoon failure on the orangutan and other rainforest animals.
- Compare the orangutan's diet with the human diet.

Glossary

Adolescent The age of animals just before they become adults.

Canine teeth Large, sharp teeth used for biting and fighting.

Carbohydrates Substances found in food that give the body energy.

Courtship The behaviour of animals that leads to mating.

Diterocarp A class of tropical trees in Asia.

Dominant The strongest animal who holds a territory.

Habitat The place where an animal or plant naturally lives.

Home range An area of land used by an animal but not defended as a territory.

Juvenile An orangutan is called a juvenile between three and five years old.

Mammal An animal that feeds its young on milk.

Nectar A sugary liquid made by flowers.

Opposable thumbs Thumbs positioned opposite the fingers, so the hand can grip.

Orphan A young animal whose parents have died.

Predator An animal that kills and eats other animals.

Proteins Substances found in food that the body needs to grow and build muscles.

Quarantine A system in which sick animals are kept apart from healthy ones.

Rehabilitation The process of returning a captive animal to the wild.

Smuggling Moving animals between countries illegally.

Species A group of animals or plants with similar features that can breed together.

Suckling Drinking a mother's milk.

Territory An area that an animal defends.

Wean A mother weans her baby when she stops it drinking her milk.

Further Information

Organisations to Contact

WWF-UK
Panda House, Weyside Park
Godalming, Surrey GU7 1XR
Tel. 01483 426444
Website: www.wwf-uk.org

The International Primate
Protection League (IPPL)
116 Judd Street
London WC1H 9NS
Tel. 0207 8330661
Website: www.ippl-uk.org

The Orangutan Foundation
7 Kent Terrace,
London NW1 4RP
Tel: 0207 7242912
Website: www.orangutan.org

Websites

Orangutan Foundation
International
www.ns.net/orangutan/
News, facts and pictures of
orangutans, including an
'Orangutan of the Month'.

Primates Online
www.primates-online.com
Information on apes and
monkeys. Includes a Kids' Club.

Books to Read

Among the Orangutans by Evelyn
Gallardo (Chronicle Books, 1995)
Apes by Tess Lemon (David
Bennett Books, 1993)
Eyewitness Gorilla by Ian
Redmond (Dorling Kindersley,
1997)

Index

All the numbers in **bold** refer to photographs or illustrations.

adolescence **22**, 23, 45
arms **5**, 9, 26, **27**

babies 8, **9**, **10**, 11, 16, 33, **38**, **41**, 42, **44**, 47
breeding 30, 32, 33, 34, 40

calls 5, 30, 32
cheek pads **5**, 25, **30**, **32**, **34**, 45
climbing 10, 11, **15**, 26, **27**, 33
coat and hair 5, 9
courtship 32, 33, 47

disease 34, 43
dominant males 32, 45, 47

eyes 4, **5**, 6, 7, 9

feet **5**, **15**, 16, 26
fighting 5, 31, 34
food and feeding 12, 15, **19**, 20, **21**, **28**, 29, 33, 42, 44

great apes **6**, **7**

hands 5, 6, 15, 16, 26, 47
height 4
home ranges 25, 31, 47

juveniles **14**, **15**, 16, 44

legs 9

mating 15, 16, 31, 32, 33

nests 8, 13, **14**, **29**, 42

old age 34

pets 38, 39, 42
predators **11**, 34
pregnancy 8, 16, 32, 44, 47

rehabilitation **42**, **43**, 47

sub-adults **25**, 45
suckling 8, **12**, 44, 47

teeth and jaws **22**, 28, **31**
territory 30, 32, 34, 45, 47
throat pouch **5**, 32

weaning 14, 44, 47
weight 4, 5, 9, 26, 32, 43

zoos 39, **40**, 41, 47